MW01230714

AS I SIT HERE...

Kathryn Whitley

This is dedicated to:

everyone who has had an impact on who I am and who I'm becoming: my family, 1004, K, and I. Thank you for pushing and challenging me.

A 'Brief' History

So I used to be a super happy person which is really crazy to think about because I've grown so used to happiness being a rarity. Back in middle school and before, I would get hyper attached to boys. If I had a crush it was all I would think about, talk about, do anything about. My brain has problems with obsession and boys were just another one. Up until senior year of high school, that's how I was. I went from having a crush on one guy to the next (hardly anyone ever liked me back). Then one day a miracle happened and a guy I liked liked me back!!! It was crazy!!! We were long distance then he transferred schools and moved like 2 miles away. Literally our first conversation was a fight and that should've been a sign. He mostly made me happy but he had this angry side that made me feel like I was always walking on eggshells. I had to be careful what I said or else he would go off. But he loved me, so that was okay, right??

We were together for two years. But we 'broke up' at least twice a month. One night I would be crying myself to sleep then the next he would be telling me he loved me. I thought this was normal. This was my first relationship; I didn't know any better. My parents were the same age when they met and were very similar to my boyfriend and I, so I figured if they could do it, so could we. One morning, I woke up and I SWORE I was pregnant. I was on birth control and had never had sex but my brain saw a little bloating and though 'yep I'm pregnant.' I would take pictures every morning and night to track the difference (food baby?). I Googled to see what symptoms I should be experiencing and what my stomach should look like (hypochondriac??). Dance was even worse because it's just me in a leotard surrounded by mirrors at every angle for five hours every week. That's already hard enough for a developing teenage girl, much less one going through this.

As if I couldn't get any worse, I stopped eating. No food means no food baby, right? I was already skinny but I still obviously lost weight. And when I did eat, I would bloat even worse which would stress me out more. My exhaustion showed in dance when I would almost pass out every class. I would buy pregnancy tests month after month. They would always be negative. I would get my period every month. But I was still convinced I was pregnant. I grew more angry and irritated the more stressed I got. This ruined my relationship with my family as well as with my boyfriend. We would fight and he would try to leave me, but I would tell him I was carrying his baby and force him to stay. I cried myself to sleep every night. I genuinely wanted to die. My parents read my diary and saw how worried and depressed I was, ruining our relationship even more. They sent me to a therapist who sucked. I've always had trouble talking about my feelings, especially to random strangers. .

After talking with my doctor and taking so many negative pregnancy tests, I was eventually convinced and started eating like normal again. I had to quit dance because I still had trouble looking at myself in the mirror and even to this day there are times when it's still hard.

I eventually started dating a senior in my AP Physics class which taught me what a happy, healthy relationship should be like. However, he didn't want to do long distance after he graduated so there was always this eminent end to our relationship. It was May and I was stressed about exams and life and got irritated very easily. He took this as him no longer making me happy, so he ended things. After, I told him he had been the one thing keeping me sane through everything, and part of me always thought we would find our way back to each other (thankfully I've moved on from that).

Post-breakup I went around flirting again. A lot. This is where our favorite person comes into play. E and I have been friends since 7th grade. We lost touch junior year, but started talking again senior year. Neither of us wanted anything serious senior year. Casual. Like that ever works. It started off fine, but we both started to catch feelings. Eventually we said the "l word" but we both knew we couldn't be with each other, yet we still hungout. I dated someone for about three months, but it always came back to E, so instead of hurting the poor guy, I left.

But E and I still couldn't be together. He had other girls and he ditched me at prom, but for some reason I stayed. We would argue and stop talking for a few weeks then one of us would cave and we would fall back together. But we both knew he was leaving and he thought a military relationship would be too hard, regardless of what I said. There was no changing his mind.

The last month before he left, he started getting really flirty and affectionate which confused me. The last time I saw him before he left, I asked what he wanted. He told me, kind of, but he was never explicit which left me even more confused. I went on dates. I downloaded Tinder. But he was always there.

I wrote him and he wrote me back in the beginning. Then he just stopped. I kept writing, but I never got a response which made me even more conflicted. Like I said before, I usually get emotionally attached to every guy I talk to, but since he left, I couldn't. I went on dates and felt absolutely nothing except possibly regret. As I continued to attempt to move on, part of me was still holding onto the hope that maybe he would still want me.

And then I met *I*. At first I thought he was just some annoying guy in my critical thinking class only trying to get with me, so I closed myself off from him. But then whenever his name would pop up in my notifications, I would get excited and I thought "oh no, it's happening." When it wasn't his name, I would get disappointed. I wasn't sure what I was to him, so I kept my distance.

But then he kissed me and I genuinely felt like I was transported to another planet; I hadn't felt that way in so long. I constantly wanted to be around him and hangout with him and talk to him. I get excited when I see his name or face. But I also get scared. I have absolutely no idea what I want relationship-wise, but I do know he makes me happy and makes me laugh and I enjoy spending time with him and talking to him and I feel like I can be myself with him. There are a lot of times when I look at him and I'm like "I could stay like this forever." But then I have bad days and I'm scared he won't like me for me or I'll fall down a rabbit hole of depression and anxiety.

I know now there is more for me out there. This is a big world, that was a small town. (There in my rearview mirror disappearing now...) I want to let go of Albany and enjoy the life that is right here in front of me.

6/2/18

I'm looking down onto the clouds right now and my heart is humbled. I am so incredibly lucky to be alive in this world and live the life I live. All my ups and downs have brought me right to this moment and made me who I am. I am loved by such an amazing God who created this beautiful universe and everything I have experienced was given to me by Him to make me stronger and hold onto faith harder. I keep thinking of a quote from *Awakenings*: "We don't ask 'why?' when we are born healthy. But we ask 'why?' when we get sick or something goes wrong." We're never grateful for the life we live until something goes wrong and then we'd give anything to go back. I've come so far from being in a dark place and wanting to die, to praying I would live another day.

6/11/18

i'm alone in our hotel room about to read and i can't stop looking out the window and trying to wrap my head around the fact that in two months i will be living here. my family won't be here, it will just be me. alone. in atlanta. it still doesn't seem real and i'm scared out of my mind. i'm hoping i come back and read this after freshman year and laugh at how silly it was that i'm nervous about the big city and growing up. i've always been drawn to cities and skyscrapers. i don't know if it's because everything is so big so i feel small and insignificant in this huge world and it allows me to lose myself in a crowd and just simply be. maybe it's being trapped in a small town for so long that i want something new and exciting and fast paced. or maybe this is where i'm meant to be. maybe this is where i come out of the oppressive shell i've been living in and i thrive. everyday will be different and new and it will scare me at first but this is about to be my home. not smalbany. not conservative lee county. but atlanta. a city full of possibilities and hope and promise. i hope i'm able to embrace this change and am able to move past my insecurities in order to experience atlanta the way it's meant to be seen.

6/29/18

I don't remember what it's like to not have this imbalance in my head. You know when you're sick with a stuffed nose and you can't remember what it's like to breathe normally? It's like that. I don't remember what it's like to breathe normally. Is this normal? Is this what I used to be? Or am I still unbalanced?

6/25/18

E and I were walking out of Break Time after I failed miserably at
playing pool. I was upset with myself and embarrassed and self-
conscious, even though I knew no one else cared how good or bad I
played pool. I was on the verge of tears, but this was what E liked to
do so I put on a smile and pretended I was enjoying every second to
make him happy. I looked at him and apologized, as I too often do, for
being horrible at pool and ruining his experience that day. He just
looked at me and said how he had had an amazing time just being
with me. The whole car ride back to his house I was still sulking and
he was trying to comfort me telling me he was worse when he first
started and that I hadn't ruined his time and we'd go back and try
again. I got home, took a nap, and I woke up and realized what
amazing people I have in my life. All the things I hate about myself,
they love me in spite of. Even with all of my fears and worries and
insecurities I am still loved by so many. So why shouldn't I love
myself in spite of these things too?

7/10/18

Music is a powerful thing. I look around while at a Sam Smith concert, and all of these strangers have come together and are sharing these same moments, yet we all have different stories and different moments we relate to songs and lyrics. It just amazes me how much words can move us and inspire us and change us.

7/24/18

I'm struggling to truly be by myself. For as long as I can remember I've had a crush or someone I was pining after or a boyfriend or a boy toy or something and I don't know how to just be me. So much of who I am is based on the validation and acceptance from others and I hate that but I also don't know how to be any different. I don't know where to start to truly find self acceptance. I say that I love myself but do I? I can't be without a guy to flirt with or talk to or call me pretty because then I feel unworthy and not good enough. I need to stop getting so attached to everyone I talk to and let life just happen to me. I need to let go and loosen the reins. But I'm lost. I feel like I'm standing in the middle of the Brooklyn Bridge and cars are just flying past me and no one notices I'm here. I don't know where to go or how to lift a foot off the ground. I keep waiting for someone to grab my hand or stop their car and take me where I need to go, but I need to stop waiting. I have to grab my own hand, get in my own car, and find my place for myself.

7/25/18

I know this is probably pretty obvious but I've just been sitting
here reflecting and thinking, I think sometimes I forget that
people I look up to like Megan and Liz and Taylor Swift are
real humans. That sounds really stupid and like "duh, Kathryn"
but like with Demi, I think sometimes we forget that these
people we look up to go through the same things we do. They
struggle with themselves and life and just because, to us, they
seem perfect and happy all the time, that doesn't make them
immune to imperfections and imbalances. I think we all want
these celebrities to be bigger and better than us because we feel
like it gives us hope, but we also need to remember that they are
imperfect humans and that's okay and we should love them
anyways, just like we should love our own imperfections
because that's what makes us us.

8/8/18

I just got back to my car after taking myself on a movie date to watch Mamma Mia. I guess it's part of my process of learning to love myself and being okay being alone. I walked in super self conscious about buying just a movie ticket for myself but the guy that sold me the tickets was super sweet and cute and reminded me that people don't think I'm a loser for seeing a movie by myself at 4pm on a Wednesday! It's okay to do things by yourself! When I walked into the theater, there were only two people in there and, once again, felt self conscious sitting by myself knowing I wasn't waiting on someone else to show up and sit next to me. But as I watched this movie about this girl traveling to Greece by herself and starting this adventure and life on her own, I learned that being alone is fun, it's empowering, it's beautiful. Now I'm sitting in my car listening to Andante, Andante while it rains from a sunny sky thinking about how I'm basically starting over on Sunday. Atlanta is my new Greece. I've got to pull myself up by my overall straps and Donna Sheridan this bitch. Am I right ladies?

8/10/18

I just left the Taylor Swift concert and I'm sitting here, two days before move-in, looking out at the city and realizing this is my new home. The newest chapter of my life is starting. It's here. And I'm starting it with Taylor and my best friends. What better way?

8/20/18

I'm sitting outside Langdale Hall in the small part of campus that actually feels like a college campus. There's a fountain and benches and ~some~ green space. If it weren't for the traffic and sirens, you might be able to forget you're in the city. I sit out here every Tuesday and Thursday while I wait for Kyla to get out of class so we can go to Critical Thinking together. I'm mostly caught up on my homework, so I've just been sitting here thinking. I come here after my neuro class and for some reason, today's class really blew my mind. The brain is such a crazy thing how it turns electrical and chemical signals into the thoughts and memories and world around us. And yet, there's so much we don't know about the brain. Which means there is so much we don't know about ourselves. How crazy is that??

8/23/18

So I've lived in this beautiful city on my own for almost two full weeks, and somehow I've survived, and somehow I'm happy. I haven't written since I've been here so I'll do a quick little update then jump into my philosophical thoughts. I've grown so close with my roommates; I made a real connection with a guy for the first time in forever and my anxiety annoyed him; I'm pushing myself to be alone and be okay with it; I'm so excited for my classes and for what the future holds for me here. Although I thought moving here would be harder than it was (trust me it's still hard), I'm actually finding myself less depressed and more excited for life and what each new day holds. It could be because I get to spend time with my amazing, hilarious roommates everyday or because I'm having to force myself to be in this moment or maybe because this is just simply the change that I've been needing. I'm still so nervous about what the future holds but living in this city surrounded by so many people and events and stories and history is teaching me to be here. Now. Not anxious about tomorrow. Not worried about what my future career may hold. But here. In this city. In each moment. Right now I am here at Georgia State and I am alive and healthy and bettering myself. (Also my favorite part about living in these dorms is hearing every time the person above me flushes lol)

10/1/18

This past week has been rough for me. I'll give you an overview.

Sunday: My dog I've had for as long as I can remember died. My love also called everyone from bootcamp but me.

Monday: I made a 60 on a chem quiz I studied 4 hours for.

Tuesday: That depression hit.

Wednesday: I said "butt" in the middle of an interview. I also broke a buret in chem and spilt NaOH all over me. I now owe the chemistry department $68.

Thursday: It started pouring rain while I was walking to class and I got stuck under the law building because the wind was pushing me over.

Friday: My boyfriend called me names.

It's been rough, but I went on a family picnic with my roommates on Sunday and as I was staring out at the city from Piedmont Park, I realized how unbelievably lucky I am. I have a great group of friends who make me laugh and make me smile way more than Prozac ever did. I've never felt so at home and so loved. I get overwhelmed at the complete 180 my life has done since I moved here. We were singing to Disney Channel songs while driving through Midtown and I've never felt so complete. I hope I'm able to feel this feeling for a long time.

10/10/18

As someone who has been through her own mental health struggles, #WorldMentalHealthDay is extremely important to me. For years I've struggled with my anxiety, depression, and body image. Even now I have bad days mixed in with my good days. And it's hard. It's hard navigating in a world that expects us to be perfect and happy and functional all the time. We are all human beings. We all have a brain that beats us up sometimes. And that's okay! We should talk about it! We should educate our children about it! We should support those in our lives who are struggling! We should ask for help when we need it! We all have a plan set up for us and, sometimes, facing a mental illness may get us where we need to be. For me, I discovered my love of psychology and neuroscience and my desire to better the lives of those suffering from autism, Alzheimer's, or mental illness. As my favorite human, Miss Swift, says "without your past, you could never have arrived-so wondrously and brutally, by design or some violent, exquisite happenstance...here."

10/22/18

It's finally starting to feel like fall outside. I was walking home
from a neuroscience conference last night with this group of girls
I had met. We walked through the heart of downtown near where
all the restaurants and big hotels are. There was a chill in the air. I
had a group of girls to laugh and talk with. I looked out at the city
lit up in front of me and felt content. Complete and utter
contentment. Everything I had been scared of, all my fears and
anxieties about the future, disappeared in that moment. For the
first time in a long time, I was truly living in the moment and was
able to laugh without fear of the future.

11/6/18

It's 1AM and I can feel it happening. I can feel myself sinking and falling back into that hole and I'm scared. I'm scared of losing the friendships I've made and the relationship I've formed. I'm scared of being rejected and pushed out of the group. I'm scared of being too much to handle. And I ask myself why. Why now? Life is going surprisingly good. Why is this creeping up on me now? But I know. The serotonin in my brain doesn't care about my fears and anxieties and happiness. It functions on its own. The brain is a parasite and it's deciding that now is the time to start feeding. Buckle up, cowboys.

11/23/18

They say distance makes the heart grow fonder. I didn't know that was true until it's midnight and the only thing I can think of is your arms around me and our smiles driving through the city at night and the way you look at me when you think I can't see you and how much I want to say that I love you, but also how scared I am that you don't feel the same.

11/30/18

We're sitting in the living room talking about our families and histories and spilling our hearts and I'm being humbled. I'm realizing now, after hearing stories of abuse and illness, how lucky I am to have grown up in the environment that I did. I grew up with parents who loved each other and loved my brother and me. They went above and beyond to make sure we had a fun and memorable childhood. Both sides of my family are functional, and I've never sat back and realized how incredibly lucky I am to have the life I have. It hurts me to see my friends hurting and all I want to do is hold them and say "it's not your fault" over and over until they believe me.

12/6/18

In two days, I will be 19. I sit here in Ebrik and wonder what my nineteenth year has in store for me. Where will it take me? Who will I become? And then I realize, I have control of that. I can decide who and what I want to be. Me.

12/8/18

18 Things I Learned at 18:

1. What you believe in matters.

2. I am in control of who I become.

3. Don't take friendships for granted.

4. Don't settle for someone who can't put up with your ticks.

5. If he wanted to see you, he'd make an effort.

6. Being different is not the same as being 'bad' or 'messed up'.

7. When you study, you get better grades (crazy, right?).

8. Online friends are a blessing.

9. When you're doing what you love, you get butterflies.

10. He is not the last you'll ever have.

11. Having fun means not worrying about everyone around you.

12. Tequila is not your friend.

13. Learn facts for yourself, rather than listening to the news or Internet.

14. Concerts are a form of alternate reality.

15. You are not your parents.

16. Bullshit is not easy to spot.

17. Voting is fun! And important!

18. Just because you're young doesn't mean you can't have an impact on the world around you - even if that world is right in your backyard.

12/11/18

Today I was supposed to go to a ballet class just for the fun of it. But I got scared. I battled with fear and let fear win. When will I stop? When will I fight for myself in this battle and overtake this fear that consumes me?

12/17/18

Little Things That Remind Me There is Still Good in the World

- someone leaving space for you to turn right

- conversations with a stranger in the drive-thru

- comfort in a familiar face in an uncomfortable situation

- his voice first thing in the morning

- the familiar hum of a hometown

1/1/19

It's a new year! I'm in Helen surrounded by my beautiful friends and wonderful boyfriend. But it all feels fake. It all feels too good to be true. Like any day now my world will just come crumbling down and the ropes to climb out of this hole I dug for myself will just be snakes again.

1/2/19

New year, new me? I'm laying in my childhood bed. In my childhood home. Wishing I could be turned back into nothing. I know the new year brings new promises and new hope with it but being back here. Being trapped. I worry I may never climb my way out of this hole.

1/6/19

Sometimes I sit here waiting for something to happen, for my life to begin then I have to remind myself - I'm here. Life is happening. Right now. This isn't a free trial. There is no second chance. There is no moment where you wake up one day and your life begins. It's happening all around you. It's scary. It's real. It's new. It's here.

1/26/19

Had a dream you called and said four weeks was too soon to move

on. Little did you know you'd been pushing me away for four

months.

1/28/19

Still doesn't feel like I live here. I look out while stuck on I-85
and brake lights look back at me, I look back on the days I'm
dreamed of being here. My mom says I would say "I'm gonna
live there one day" every time we'd see the skyline in the
distance. Now here I am. Right in the middle. Happy. Content.
Finding my way.

2/18/19

My grandma's cancer recently came back even stronger. As of now, there is no treatment or cure. After I got the phone call from my mom, I laid in bed until 2:30AM crying out to God and asking Him why. Asking Him why her? Why now? Why can't she have more time? We always expect Him to give us good things in life and always ask why when something goes wrong. How do we overcome this? How do we change our expectations from all good to believing in His plan?

3/18/19

I give so much for someone who receives so little.

3/21/19

Sometimes I regret hating my childhood.

I regret rushing through every moment.

I regret trying to get out of here.

I regret pressing fast-forward instead of living in the moment.

I regret not taking in the calmness and quaintness of the world around me.

But there's nothing I can do now. It's all in the past. All that I can do is take advantage of the moment I'm in.

3/26/19

Quick shoutout to my official and honorary roommates. In high school I had a rough time when it came to the social scene. Don't get me wrong, I had friends and they were great but I never seemed to fit in anywhere and feel wanted and included in larger social situations. I feel like I've finally found my niche and I'm so so grateful for them.

4/27/19

What am I missing out on?

What if this isn't it?

What if there's someone else?

What experiences will I never have?

What if we tried?

What if we didn't?

What if I stayed?

What if I left?

What do I do?

5/5/19

I'm lost.

I'm lost and I don't know what I want.

Everything is changing again.

It always seems to happen all at once

And with no warning.

I've learned to go with the flow, but I still wonder

Where is the flow taking me?

What will be waiting for me at the end of this stream?

5/7/19

So I'm done with my first 'official' year in college. And what a year it has been.

I've made friends and I've lost friends.

I've fallen in and out of love.

I've received phone calls that have crushed me.

I've received text messages that have stayed with me all day.

I've learned to love myself.

I've also become Tik Tok famous, check me out @prettyuglykitty

CPSIA information can be obtained
at www.ICGtesting.com
Printed in the USA
LVHW070442230720
661014LV00029B/736